D1474134

The Tragedy of White Injustice and Other Meditations

The Tragedy of White Injustice and Other Meditations

Marcus Garvey

MINT EDITIONS

The Tragedy of White Injustice and Other Meditations was first published in 1927.

This edition published by Mint Editions 2023.

ISBN 9781513137711 | E-ISBN 9781513138015

Published by Mint Editions®

 MINT
EDITIONS

minteditionbooks.com

Publishing Director: Jennifer Newens
Design & Production: Rachel Lopez Metzger
Project Manager: Micaela Clark
Typesetting: Westchester Publishing Services

Dedicated
To the international membership of the Universal Negro
Improvement Association and the honest and honorable of
the human race who love truth for truth's sake, with the hope
of bettering a vicious, vain and corrupt humanity.

Contents

The Tragedy of White Injustice

(1)

Lying and stealing is the white man's game
For rights of God nor man he has no shame
(A practice of his throughout the whole world)
At all, great thunderbolts he has hurled;
He has stolen everywhere—land and sea;
A buccaneer and pirate he must be,
Killing all, as he roams from place to place,
Leaving disease, mongrels—moral disgrace.

(2)

The world's history of him is replete,
From his javelin-bolt to new-built fleet:
Hosts he has robbed and crushed below;
Of friend and neighbor he has made a foe.
From our men and women he made the slave,
Then boastingly he calls himself brave;
Cowardly, he steals on his trusting prey,
Killing in the dark, then shouts he hoo ray!

(3)

Not to go back to time prehistoric,
Only when men in Nature used to frolic,
And you will find his big, long murder-list,
Showing the plunderings of his mailed fist;
Africa, Asia and America
Tell the tale in a mournful replica
How tribesmen, Indians and Zulus fell
Fleeing the murdering bandit pell mell.

(4)

American Indian tribes were free,
Sporting, dancing, and happy as could be;
Asia's hordes lived then a life their own,
To civilization they would have grown;
Africa's millions laughed with the sun,
In the cycle of man a course to run;
In stepped the white man, bloody and grim,
The light of these people's freedom to dim.

(5)

Coolies of Asiatics they quickly made,
In Africa's blacks they built a world trade,
The Red Indians they killed with the gun,
All else of men and beasts they put to run;
Blood of murderer Cain is on their head,
Of man and beast they mean to kill dead;
A world of their own is their greatest aim,
For which Yellow and Black are well to blame.

(6)

Out of cold old Europe these white men came,
From caves, dens, and holes, without any fame,
Eating their dead's flesh and sucking their blood,
Relics of the Mediterranean flood;
Literature, science and art they stole,
After Africa had measured each pole,
Asia taught them what great learning was,
Now they frown upon what the Coolie does.

(7)

They have stolen, murdered, on their way here,
Leaving desolation and waste everywhere;
Now they boastingly tell what they have done,
Seeing not the bloody crown they have won;

Millions of Blacks died in America,
Coolies, peons, serfs, too, in Asia;
Upon these dead bones Empires they builded,
Parceling out crowns and coronets gilded.

(8)

Trifling with God's Holy Name and Law,
Mixing Christ's religion that had no flaw,
They have dared to tell us what is right,
In language of death-bullets, gas and might
Only with their brute force they hold us down,
Men of color, Yellow, Red, Black and Brown:
Not a fair chance give they our men to rise,
Christian liars we see in their eyes.

(9)

With the Bible they go to foreign lands,
Taking Christ and stealth in different hands;
Making of God a mockery on earth,
When of the Holy One there is no dearth:
They say to us: "You, sirs, are the heathen,
"We your brethren-Christian fellowmen,
"We come to tell the story of our God";
When we believe, they give to us the rod.

(10)

After our confidence they have thus won,
From our dear land and treasure we must run;
Story of the Bible no more they tell,
For our souls redeemed we could go to hell.
Oil, coal and rubber, silver and gold,
They have found in wealth of our lands untold:
Thus, they claim the name of our country, all,
Of us they make then their real football.

(11)

If in the land we happen to tarry,
Most of us then become sad and sorry,
For a white man's country they say it is,
And with shot, gas and shell, they prove it his:
What can we do who love the Gracious Lord,
But fight, pray, watch and wait His Holy word:
His second coming we know to be true,
Then, He will greet the white man with his due.

(12)

This Christ they killed on Calvary's Cross,
After His Person around they did toss:
White men the Savior did crucify,
For eyes not blue, but blood of Negro tie;
Now they worship Him in their churches great,
And of the Holy Ghost they daily prate;
"One God" they say, enough for all mankind,
When in slavery the Blacks they entwined.

(13)

Their churches lines of demarcation draw;
In the name of Christ there is no such law,
Yet Black and White they have separated,
A Jim Crow God the preachers operated,
Then to Heaven they think they will all go,
When their consciences ought to tell them No.
God is no respecter of persons great,
So each man must abide his final fate.

(14)

We'd like to see the white man converted,
And to right and justice be devoted;
Continuing in land-values to lie and steal,
Will bring destruction down upon his heel.

All that the other races want, I see,
Is the right to liberty and be free:
This the selfish white man doesn't want to give;
He alone, he thinks, has the right to live.

(15)

There shall be a bloody mix-up everywhere;
Of the white man's plunder we are aware:
Men of color the great cause understand,
Unite they must, to protect their own land.
No fool's stand on argument must we make:
Between Heaven and earth an oath we take:
"Our lands to deliver from foreign foes,
Caring not of trials and maudlin woes."

(16)

The privilege of men to protect home
Was established before the days of Rome.
Many gallant races fought and died,
Alien hordes in triumph thus defied.
Carthage did not crush Ancient Greece
For their believing in the Golden Fleece.
No other race shall kill the sturdy Blacks
If on their tribal gods we turn our backs.

(17)

From Marathon, Tours, Blenheim and the Marne
A braver courage in man has been born;
Africans died at Thermopylae's Pass,
Standing firm for Persia-men of Brass.
The Black Archers of Ethiopia stood
At Marathon, proving their stern manhood;
Senegalese held their own at Verdun,
Even though their praises are not now sung.

(18)

In the Americas' modern warfare
The Blacks have ever borne their share;
With Cortez, Washington, too, and the rest,
We did for the others our truthful best;
At St. Domingo we struck a clear blow.
To show which way the wind may one day go.
Toussaint L'Ouverture was our leader then,
At the time when we were only half-men.

(19)

Italians, Menelik put to chase,
Beating a retreat in uneven haste;
So down the line of history we come,
Black, courtly, courageous and handsome.
No fear have we today of any great men
From Napoleon back to Genghis Khan;
All we ask of men is "Give a square deal,"
Returning to others same right we feel.

(20)

With a past brilliant, noble and grand,
Black men march to the future hand in hand;
We have suffered long from the white man's greed,
Perforce he must change his unholy creed.
Stealing, bullying and lying to all
Will drag him to ignominious fall;
For men are wise—yes, no longer are fools,
To have grafters make of them still cheap tools.

(21)

Each race should be proud and stick to its own,
And the best of what they are should be shown;
This is no shallow song of hate to sing,
But over Blacks there should be no white king,

Every man on his own foothold should stand,
Claiming a nation and a Fatherland!
White, Yellow and Black should make their own laws,
And force no one-sided justice with flaws.

(22)

Man will bear so much of imposition,
Till he starts a righteous inquisition.
History teaches this as a true fact,
Upon this premise all men do act.
Sooner or later each people take their stand
To fight against the strong, oppressive hand;
This is God's plan, raising man to power,
As over sin and greed He makes him tower.

(23)

This trite lesson the white man has not learnt,
Waiting until he gets his fingers burnt.
Milleniums ago, when white men slept,
The great torch of light Asia kept.
Africa at various periods shone
Above them all as the bright noonday sun;
Coming from the darkened cave and hut,
The white man opened the gate that was shut.

(24)

Gradually light bore down upon him,
This ancient savage who was once dim;
When he commenced to see and move around,
He found the book of knowledge on the ground;
Centuries of wonder and achievements
Were cast before him in God's compliments;
But, like the rest, he has now fallen flat,
And must in the Lord's cycle yield for that.

(25)

We shall always be our brother's keeper,
Is the injunction of the Redeemer;
Love and tolerance we must ever show,
If in Grace Divine we would truly grow;
This is the way clear to God's great kingdom
Not by the death-traps of Argonne or Somme,
When the terrible white man learns this much,
He will save even the African Dutch.

(26)

South Africa has a grave problem now
In reducing the Negro to the plow;
White men are to live in their lazy ease
While the patience of the goodly natives tease;
They make new laws to have Africa white
Precipitating righteous and ready fight:
Around the world they speak of being so just,
Yet, in fact, no lone white man can you trust.

(27)

In Australia the same they have done,
And so, wherever man's confidence won:
This they call the religion of the Christ,
And upon their willing slave try to foist.
Only a part of the world can you fool,
And easily reduce to your foot-stool;
The other one-half is always awake,
And from it you cannot liberty take.

(28)

"And now valiant Black men of the west
Must ably rise to lead and save the rest":
This is the ringing call Africa sounds,
As throughout the Godly world it resounds;

Clansmen! black, educated, virile and true!
Let us prove too that we are loyal blue.
We must win in the blessed fight of love,
Trusting on the Maker of men above.

(29)

The Christian world is yet to be saved!
Man, since the risen Christ has not behaved!
Wanton, reckless, wicked, he still remains,
Causing grief, sorrow, tears and human pains!
Can we show the Godly light to anyone
Seeking for earnest truth while marching on?
If so, friend, let us tell you now and here,
For love, freedom, justice let's all prepare!

(30)

God in His Glorious Might is coming,
Wonderful signs He is ever showing,
Unrest, earthquakes, hurricanes, floods and storms
Are but revelations of Heavenly Forms:
The proud white scientist thinks he is wise
But the Black man's God comes in true disguise,
God is sure in the rumbling earthquake,
When He is ready, the whole world will shake.

(31)

The Armageddon is gathering now;
The sign is on every oppressed man's brow:
The whites who think they are ever so smart
Do not know other men can play their part:
When the opportune time is almost here
Black, Yellow and Brown will be ev'rywhere,
In union of cause they'll stand together
And storms of the bully boldly weather.

(32)

Their gases and shots, and their rays of death,
Shall only be child's play-a dream of Seth,
For out of the clear, sleeping minds of ages,
Wonders shall be written on history's pages:
Our buried arts and sciences then shall rise,
To show how for centuries we were wise:
Silent tongues we kept, by God's true command,
Until of us, action, He did demand.

(33)

Under the canopy of Nature's law
We shall unitedly and bravely draw.
On the plains of God's green Amphitheatre,
Swords, in rhythm with Divine Meter:
Jehovah's Day will have surely come,
With Angelic strains and Seraphic hum:
The Guides of Heaven will direct the way,
Keeping us from wandering far astray.

(34)

Like around the high walls of Jericho,
March we, as Rio speeds through Mexico:
Trumpets loud will the Guiding Angels blow.
As scatter the enemy to-and-fro:
Heaven will have given us a battle cry:
"Oh Brave Soldiers you shall never die":
Rally to the command of Heaven's King,
As Cherubim to Him your tidings bring.

(35)

See the deadly clash of arms! Watch!
They fall! There is stillness!—It is the funeral pall!
A sad requiem now is to be sung!
Not by Angels, but in their human tongue!

The cruel masters of yest'rday are done!
From the fields of battle they have run!
A brand new world of justice is to be!
"You shall be a true brother unto me!"

(36)

This is a forecast of God's wrath:
White man, will you turn from the evil path?
There is still hope for you, among the good:
If you will seek the bigger-brotherhood:
Stop your tricks, frauds, lying and stealing,
And settle down to fair and square dealing:
If not, prepare yourself for gloomy hell,
As God announces the sorrowing knell.

(37)

Your lies, to us called diplomacy,
Are known by us, a brazen phantasy;
You imprison men for crimes not so great,
While on your silly wisdom you do prate.
The masses are soberly watching you;
They know that you are false and so untrue.
The laborers of your race you oppress,
As well as black and other men you distress.

(38)

If you were wise you'd read between the lines
Of feudal isms and others of old times.
Men have fought against ugly royal gods,
Burying them 'neath European sods.
Such to heartless masters the people do,
From Syracuse to bloody Waterloo;
Wonderful lessons for any sober man,
Who worships not idols or the god Pan.

(39)

In the vicious order of things today,
The poor, suffering black man has no say;
The plot is set for one 'gainst the other,
With organization they mustn't bother.
"If one should show his head as a leader,
Whom we cannot use, the rest to pilfer,
We shall discredit him before his own,
And make of him a notorious clown."

(40)

"In Africa we have plans to match him,
While the native Chiefs of their lands we trim;
The Blacks schooled in England are too smart,
On the I Better Than You scheme we'll start,
And have them thinking away from the rest:
This philosophy for them is best—
Easier then we can rob the good lands
And make ourselves rich without soiled hands."

(41)

"We will so keep from them the 'Negro World'
That no news they'll have of a flag unfurled:
Should they smuggle copies in, and we fail,
We will send the sly agents all to jail."
This is the white man's plan across the sea.
Isn't this wily and vicious as can be?
In other lands they have things arranged
Differently, yet they have never changed.

(42)

In America they have Colored to tell
What they know of the rest, whose rights they sell;
The Blacks they do try to keep always down,
But in time they will reap what they have sown.

No Negro's good life is safe in the STATES
If he tries to be honest with his mates;
In politics he must sell at the polls,
To suit the white man in his many roles.

(43)

The West Indian whites are tricky, too;
They have schemes curved like the horse's shoe:
There is only one opening for the black—
Three other sides are close up to his back;
Hence he never gets a chance to look in
Whilst staring at the world of mortal sin.
Yes, this is the game they play everywhere,
Leaving the Negro to gloom and despair.

(44)

And now, white man, can we reason with you,
For each race in the world to give it due?
Africa for Africans is most right;
Asia for Asiatics is light;
To Europe for the Europeans,
America for the Americans:
This is the doctrine of the goodly Klan,
Now fighting for the alien ban.

(45)

Blacks do not hate you because you are white;
We believe in giving to all men right;
Some we do keep for ourselves to protect,
Knowing it as a virtue to select.
We are willing to be friends of mankind,
Pulling all together with none behind,
Growing in sane goodness and fellowship,
Choosing but the Almighty to worship.

(46)

Let justice prevail, at home and abroad;
Cease over the weak your burdens to lord;
You're but mortal man, like the rest of us—
Of this happy truth we need make no fuss.
All Nature's kindly gifts are justly ours—
Suns, oceans, trees, to pretty flowers—
So we need not doubt the marvelous fact
That God has given to each man his tract.

(47)

The common thief now steals a crust of bread,
The law comes down upon his hungry head;
The haughty land robber steals continents,
With men, oil, gold, rubber and all contents.
The first you say is a hopeless convic',
While the latter escapes the law by trick;
That grave, one-sided justice will not do—
The poor call for consideration, too.

(48)

The rich white man starts the unholy war,
Then from the line of action he keeps far;
He pushes to the front sons of the poor,
There to do battle, die, suffer galore,
As the guns rage, liberty loans they raise,
And in glorious tones sing freedom's praise.
This is the method to gain them more wealth,
Then, after vict'ry they practice great stealth.

(49)

Those who make wars should first go to the front,
And of gas, shot and shell hear there the brunt:
In first lines of action they are all due,
If to their country and people they are true:

When this is demanded in right of all,
There will be no more deadly cannon ball:
The downtrodden poor whites and blacks should join
And prevent rich whites our rights to purloin.

(50)

Weeping mothers, tricked in patriotism,
Send their sons to fight for liberalism:
Into most far off lands they go with pride,
Thinking right and God be on their side:
When they get into the bloody trenches,
They find of lies they had awful drenches:
The people they were all supposed to kill,
Like themselves, had gotten of lies their fill.

(51)

In the private club and drawing room,
White schemes are hatched for the nation's doom:
Speculators, grafters, bankers-all,
With politicians join to hasten the fall,
By stealing rights from other citizens,
As if they weren't fit or true denizens:
How awful is this daring story
That we tell to men young and hoary.

(52)

Crooked lawyers, friends and politicians,
Corrupt the morals of the good nations:
Between them and others, fly plots they make,
Large fees they charge, to have you surely broke,
Innocent citizens' money to take;
From banks they find out your real account,
Then have you indicted on legal count:
Then, to prison you go-what a sad joke!

The white man controls cable and wireless,
Connections by ships with force and duress:
He keeps black races of the world apart,
So to his schemes they may not be smart:
"There shall be no Black Star Line Ships," he says,
"For that will interfere with our crooked ways:
"I'll disrupt their business and all their plans,
"So they might not connect with foreign lands."

Black women are raped by the lordly white,
In colonies, the shame ne'er reaching light:
In other countries abuses are given,
Shocking to morality and God's Heaven.
Hybrids and mongrels are the open result,
Which the whites give us as shameful insult:
How can they justify this? None can tell:
Yet, crimes of the blacks are rung with a bell.

White men newspapers subsidize and own,
For to keep them on their racial throne:
Editors are slaves to fool the public,
Reporters tell the lie and pull the trick;
The papers support only what they want,
Yet truth, fair play, and justice, daily flaunt:
They make criminals out of honest men,
And force judges to send them to the Pen.

Capitalists buy up all blank space
To advertise and hold the leading place
For to influence public opinion
And o'er Chief-editors show dominion.

The average man is not wise to the scheme,
He, the reformer, must now redeem;
This isn't a smooth or very easy job,
For, you, of your honor and name, they'll rob.

(57)

The bankers employ men to shoot and kill,
When we interfere with their august will;
They take the savings of deaf, dumb and poor,
Gamble with it here and on foreign shore:
In oil, gold, rum, rubber they speculate,
Then bring their foreign troubles upon the State:
Friends in Government they control at will;
War they make, for others, our sons to kill.

(58)

The many foundations of researches,
And the foreign missions and their churches,
Are organized to catch the mild converts
Who don't understand the way of perverts.
Our wealth when discovered by researchers,
In lands of the Native occupiers
Is surveyed and marked to the river's rim
Till they dislodge a Premprey or Abd-El-Krim.

(59)

It is not freedom from prison we seek;
It is freedom from the big thieves we meet;
All life is now a soulless prison cell,
A wild suspense between heaven and hell:
Selfish, wicked whites have made it so;
To the Author and Finisher we'll go,
Carrying our sad cares and many wrongs
To Him in prayers and holy songs.

This is the game that is played all around,
Which is sure one day to each race rebound:
The world is gone mad with the money craze,
Leaving the poor man in a gloomy haze:
There must be world reorganization,
To save the masses from exploitation;
The cry is for greater democracy.
A salvation from man's hypocrisy.

(61)

Out in this heartless, bitter oasis
There's now very little of human bliss;
The cold capitalists and money sharks
Have made life unsafe, like ocean barks.
The once dear, lovely Garden of Eden
Has become the sphere of men uneven;
The good God created but an equal pair,
Now man has robbed others of their share.

(62)

Shall there be freedom of liberal thought?
No; the white man has all agencies bought
Press, pulpit, law and every other thing
Hence o'er public opinion he reigns king.
This is indisputable, glaring fact;
You may find it out with a little tact.
College tutors and presidents are paid,
So that in universities schemes are laid.

(63)

Cleopatra, Empress Josephine,
Were black mongrels like of the Philippine:
Mixtures from black and other races they,
Yet "true" the white man's history will not say

To those who seek the light of pure knowledge
In the inquiring world, school or college.
Napoleon fell for a Negro woman;
So did the Caesars, and the Great Roman.

(64)

Anthony lost his imperial crown
To escape Cleo's fascinating frown.
This truth the New Negro knows very well,
And to his brothers in darkness he'll tell.
No one can imprison the brain of man
That was never intended in God's plan;
You may persecute, starve, even debase
That will not kill truth nor virtue efface.

(65)

The white man now enjoys his "Vanity Fair";
He thinks of self and not of others care
Fratricidal course, that to hell doth lead
This is poison upon which the gentry feed.
Blacks should study physics, chemistry, more,
While the gold God all such sinners adore;
This is no idle prattle talk to you;
It has made the banners red, white and blue.

(66)

Out of the clear of God's Eternity
Shall rise a kingdom of Black Fraternity;
There shall be conquests o'er militant forces;
For as man proposes, God disposes.
Signs of retribution are on every hand:
Be ready, black men, like Gideon's band.
They may scoff and mock at you today,
But get you ready for the awful fray.

In the fair movement of God's Abounding Grace
There is a promised hope for the Negro race;
In the sublimest truth of prophecy,
God is to raise them to earthly majesty,
Princes shall come out of Egypt so grand,
The noble black man's home and Motherland,
The Psalmist spoke in holy language clear,
As Almighty God's triune will declare.

(68)

In their conceit they see not their ruin;
You soldiers of trust, be up and doing!
Remember Belshazzar's last joyous feast,
And Daniel's vision of the Great Beast!
"Weighed in the balances and found wanting"
Is the Tekel to which they are pointing.
This interpretation of the Prophet
Black men shall never in their dreams forget.

(69)

The resplendent rays of the morning sun
Shall kiss the Negro's life again begun;
The music of God's rhythmic natural law
Shall stir Afric's soul without Divine flaw.
The perfume from Nature's rosy hilltops
Shall fall on us spiritual dewdrops.
Celestial beings shall know us well,
For, by goodness, in death, with them we'll dwell.

(70)

And How Sad A Finis!

With battleship, artillery and gun
White men have put all God's creatures to run;

Heaven and earth they have often defied,
Taking no heed of the rebels that died.
God can't be mocked in this daring way,
So the evil ones shall sure have their day.
"You may rob, you may kill, for great fame,"
So says the white man, FOR THIS IS HIS GAME.

A Summer's Dream

As I lay asleep at midnight,
  A thought came stealing over me:
A shadow of a great disaster,
  The passing of my Love at sea.

I heard the chimes of Angelus,
  It sounded sad but ringing clear;
I had a glimpse of dear heaven,
  For my Love was a-going there.

The ship was lost in the ocean,
  As the storm had raged and past;
Every soul was clothed in sadness,
But my Love was firm to the last.

I stretched my arms out to rescue,
  But my Love was already gone:
A burning light stopped my vision,
  It was like shining glare at morn.

There were Angels in the Heavens,
  And sunny flowers strewn around;
The singing of Royal Cherubs
  Had a pleasing Heavenly sound.

I can almost see how clearly,
  There is a passage made above;
The Angels are a-welcoming
  The spirit of my dearest Love.

I am left with my dreams, alone,
  In a cold world of sin and care,
For my Love is gone forever,
  With happy Angels, bliss to share.

I tried to enter into Heaven.
  But the gates were closed to me;
The Guardian of my destiny
    Had not then set my spirit free.

I struggled still with the vision,
  For it was a-torturing me;
My Love was taken to Heaven,
    And the sweet face I could not see.

At last I came to my senses,
  I found it was a summer's dream;
My Love was still right beside me,
    A creature perfect as could seem.

Feb. 24, 1927

THE CITY STORM

I stood at attention to see there was an angry thunder clap!

A natural manifestation of the ugly clouds above!
Proud man was all in excitement, questioning the meaning of darkness
That surrounded him on every side, from mother earth to heaven!
Men were looking through closed windows with stares of anxiety!
Mothers were seeking their children for closer union of love!
All motive power in the city had come to a sudden stop!
There was nothing cheerful, only gloom and prehistoric weirdness!

It was not the end of all time, nor the hour for Gabriel's horn:
It was atmospheric change, caused through elemental moodiness,
That sometimes make us feel that our sciences are but speculations,
And the majesty of man, feeble, as his finite intellect:
Yet, there was a fear and trembling as I observed it all around!
Hearts were searched and prayers were offered in devout holiness!
Everyone thought it was the end of the world, the great Judgment
    morn—
The final visitation of God upon man's vain damnations!

I wondered to myself when I saw the weakness of my brother
In the moment of apparent danger and infinite distress,
How is it he finds heart to enslave the rest of his fellow men,
When conscience must tell him withal, we are in reality one?
Those heavy clouds or roaring Heaven did not gather all in vain!
On that day millions saw the evil of their fellows to oppress,
The commonness of love and punishment from the Everlasting Father
Who saves cities, nations and peoples for even the righteous ten!

After several blasts of thunder had shaken the trembling earth,
The rain from the very clouds burst through in torrential showers!
Again there was a sudden breaking of the angry elements!
A stillness, as of death, seemed to reign on every hand and shadow!
The sun, in munificent glory shone radiantly once more;
Everything was refreshed, from the green grass to the rosy flowers!

It was as if Nature had served her elemental sacraments,
To give new life to the ancient hill, dale, mountain and meadow!

But I was satisfied that in the approach of death, men unite
To shield themselves by thought and deed from the dread and
    ominous terror!
This was only a storm with its currents of electricity!
Yet the whole populace was aroused to see man's finite weakness,
To realize that in the midst of life we are subjects of death,
Children of an understanding Source, hidden beyond Nature's mirror!
Whether of men we be divided in Yellow, Brown, Black or White,
We shall pass from life to the mysterious eternity!

February 25, 1927

The Black Woman

Black queen of beauty, thou hast given color to the world!
Among other women thou art royal and the fairest!
Like the brightest of jewels in the regal diadem,
Shin'st thou, Goddess of Africa, Nature's purest emblem!

Black men worship at thy virginal shrine of truest love,
Because in thine eyes are virtue's steady and holy mark,
As we see in no other, clothed in silk or fine linen,
From ancient Venus, the Goddess, to mythical Helen.

When Africa stood at the head of the elder nations,
The Gods used to travel from foreign lands to look at thee:
On couch of costly Eastern materials, all perfumed,
Reclined thee, as in thy path flow'rs were strewn—sweetest
    that bloomed.

Thy transcendent marvelous beauty made the whole world mad,
Bringing Solomon to tears as he viewed thy comeliness;
Anthony and the elder Caesars wept at thy royal feet,
Preferring death than to leave thy presence, their foes to meet.

You, in all ages, have attracted the adoring world,
And caused many a bloody banner to be unfurled:
You have sat upon exalted and lofty eminence,
To see a world fight in your ancient African defense.

Today you have been dethroned, through the weakness of your men,
While, in frenzy, those who of yore craved your smiles and your hand-
Those who were all monsters and could not with love approach you-
Have insulted your pride and now attack your good virtue.

Because of disunion you became mother of the world,
Giving tinge of robust color to five continents,
Making a greater world of millions of colored races,
Whose claim to beauty is reflected through our black faces.

From the handsome Indian to European brunette,
There is a claim for that credit of their sunny beauty
That no one can e'er to take from thee, O Queen of all women
Who have borne trials and troubles and racial burden.

Once more we shall, in Africa, fight and conquer for you,
Restoring the pearly crown that proud Queen Sheba did wear:
Yea, it may mean blood, it may mean death; but still we shall fight,
Bearing our banners to Vict'ry, men of Afric's might.

Superior Angels look like you in Heaven above,
For thou art fairest, queen of the seasons, queen of our love:
No condition shall make us ever in life desert thee,
Sweet Goddess of the ever green land and placid blue sea.

February 28, 1927

The Black Mother

Where can I find love that never changes
    Smiles that are true and always just the same,
Caring not how the fierce tempest rages,
    Willing ever to shield my honored name?

This I find at home, only with Mother,
    Who cares for me with patient tenderness;
She from every human pain would rather
    Save me, and drink the dregs of bitterness.

If on life's way I happen to flounder,
    My true thoughts should be of Mother dear,
She is the rock that ne'er rifts asunder,
    The cry of her child, be it far or near.

This is love wonderful beyond compare;
    It is God's choicest gift to mortal man;
You, who know Mother, in this thought must share,
    For, she, of all, is Angel of your Clan.

My Mother is black, loveliest of all;
    Yes, she is as pure as the new made morn;
Her song of glee is a clear rythmic call
    To these arms of love to which I was born.

I shall never forget you, sweet Mother,
    Where'er in life I may happen to roam;
Thou shalt always be the Fairy Charmer
    To turn my dearest thoughts to things at home.

February 28, 1927

Keep Cool

Suns have set and suns will rise
Upon many gloomy lives;
Those who sit around and say:
"Nothing good comes down our way."
Some say: "What's the use to try,
Life is awful hard and dry."
If they'd bring such news to you,
This is what you ought to do.

(Chorus)

Let no trouble worry you;
Keep cool, keep cool!
Don't get hot like some folk do,
Keep cool, keep cool!
What's the use of prancing high
While the world goes smiling by.
You can win if you would try,
Keep cool, keep cool.

Throw your troubles far away,
Smile a little everyday,
And the sun will start to shine,
Making life so true and fine.
Do not let a little care
Fill your life with grief and fear:
Just be calm, be brave and true,
Keep your head and you'll get through.

(Chorus)

Let no trouble worry you;
Keep cool, keep cool!
just be brave and ever true;

Keep cool, keep cool!
If they'd put you in a flame,
Though you should not bear the blame,
Do not start to raising cane,
Keep cool, keep cool.

April 30, 1927

The Bravest Soul

The toil of life is never ending:
    It passes from one stage to others;
We live beneath its sombre bending,
    And ape the customs of our fathers.

We glory in its radiant jovs,
    And smile with the everlasting sun:
This eternal change that man emplovs.
    Has been so from Adam's day begun.

The bravest soul truly conquers all.
    In seeing God in our fellow man:
This planet is just a spinning ball
    Of God's wondrous spiritual p'an.

In this life we may know no better:
    But in death we pass to Spirit Land.
Where the Soul is free from all fetter,
    To join God in His creative hand.

August 22, 1927

Music in My Soul

There's music in my soul today,
    A joy of heart not there before:
This state of conscience I relay
    To rich and proud and meek and poor

There's music in my happy Soul:
    From Heaven's realm doth truly flow
This music in my happy Soul,
    My conscience tells me rightly so.

My song of joy I sing to you:
    Let peace and love forever be
Among ye men of every hue,
    Of every land and charted sea.

I crave no other fortune great,
    But joy to live in peace with God;
My hopes are fixed on His Estate,
    In faith so true as prophets had.

This music in my soul today
    I spread in truth with love unfurled;
On waves of cheer it goes, I pray,
To reach around the belted world.

August 23, 1927

God in Man

O weary son of sorrow great!
    How apt art thou to bow and grieve,
And count all things thy solemn fate,
    As if thou canst not self retrieve!

May I not tell the story true
    Of that Eternal Force that is—
The Force that makes the world and you;
    The Force that rules and ever lives?

Thou art the living force in part,
    The Spirit of the Mighty I;
The God of Heaven and your heart
    Is Spirit that can never die.

You're what you are in heart and mind,
    Because you will it so to be;
The man who tries himself to find,
    Is light to all, and great is he.

In each and everyone is God,
    In everything atomic life;
There is no death beneath the sod,
    This fact, not knowing, brings the strife.

August 26, 1927

Man's Immortality

Eternal is my lease on life,
If courage I can find to live.
My soul and mind are both in one,
And Nature but my elder self,
Of all I see I am the lord,
Including earth and stars and sea:
From time immemorial I'd been
A part of Almighty God.

He was the Other Self of me,
The All in One, and I a part.
There is no life without my own,
And there's no life without the God:
He is the Source of all you see
Divine, but I a part of Him.

September 13, 1927

MERRY CHRISTMAS

Christmas has a charm so dear,
Coming once for every year,
Bringing Christ in thought anew
With my greeting true to you.

For the everlasting truths
Men may differ in their views;
Still, at Xmas, it's all right
"Merry Christmas" to recite.

October 4, 1927

The Call of Heaven

I've come to learn the story
Of Jesus in His bright glory:
That home for sinners set so free
By love for you and love for me.

I bow to Thee, Son most Holy;
In truth Thou art King of Glory.
So save my soul and make me good
That I may be where Eli stood.

Thy journey through grim Bethany
Led to the Cross' sad agony:
But now Thou art the Lord of Host.
The Father, Son and Holy Ghost.

Now send to me, Light of Glory.
The message good, true and holy;
For I am ready now for home,
No longer in this vale to roam.

October 8, 1927

CHRIST THE WAY

Oh, with the Spirit as of old,
    I chant a prayer to my God;
The Being, precious, more than gold
    That Croesus has ever had.

I lift my soul to Him above,
    And sing the angels' happy praise;
The song of life in joy of love
    That men from earth to Heaven raise.

There's joy in Paradise for me,
    Although a weary child of sin;
The penitent on Calv'ry's tree
    May find the way to enter in.

My hopes are good, in Christ, the Lord;
    On Him I rest my cares of heart;
He will so bridge the Heavenly Ford
    To show the way ere I depart.

October 8, 1927

The Wicked Dies

There's a plot for you and one for me.
  Out in God's acre, that's lying by;
You needn't think I cannot also see
  That the wicked shall most surely die.

In the resurrection men shall rise
  Not those, steeped in sin and lies,
But the souls of love for good and truth
  Shall blossom forth in spiritual youth.

October 18, 1927

The World and You

The world is cold and terrible, you know,
Experience has taught the trav'ler so:
We journey from our native coast to coast,
To find little of which to gloat or boast.

However, if we trust our Conscience's Guide,
We sure shall have the truth and God beside:
This Urge of destiny is Nature's light,
It ne'er shall go astray if followed right.

October 18, 1927

You and Me

When we think of all the care
    That made life's burden great,
We long for the passing year
    To close our sad book of Fate:
But if we should stop a while,
    And think once the other way,
Life would be just all a smile,
    As we go on day by day.

We should never make day night
    For to darken life's good view;
Round that turning is the light
    That shines as a guide to you:
Think of all that's really good,
    Then make it your daily rule;
Smile with Nature's Brotherhood,
    And none make your footstool.

A proverb for everyday,
    And one more for each goodnight,
Should make life so pleasant, yea,
    Would lead us to live all right:
Turn not from sane rectitude,
    But make life just like a song;
Go ye not with the multitude
    To any path that's wholly wrong.

October 24, 1927

Man to Man

Yes, man to man is so unjust
Until we know not whom to trust;
For we have made of life a lie,
In treating man less than a fly:
To tell the reason why it's so,
Into history we must go,
Revealing crime, just after crime,
From Cain and Abel to this time.

Our God made man in perfect form,
And to the standard to conform;
But in his ways of self alone
He crushed the good and built a throne:
A regal personage is he,
As proud and selfish as can be;
Forgetting God he robs and kills,
And lays the course of human ills.

Is there no help that we can give
To brighten life in truth to live?
Yes, there is much for you to do
In treating man as Christ did you:
If we should change the old bad way,
The good would shine in us each day,
Then life would be a happy dream,
A radiant, fair morning beam.

October 25, 1927

Find Yourself

All men have troubles of their own,
    And burdens great to bear each day,
So keep your tales of woe, and frown
    At all the ills that come your way:
You need not harbor sorry pain,
    And make the world a living hell;
For there is naught in this to gain;
    The wisdom of the age will tell.

The other fellow does not care
    A bit, what ails and worries you;
In life he has to pay his fare
    In living right as you should do:
He bears his burdens like a man,
    And smiles with every wind;
There is a reason why he can
    Thus master right his soul and mind.

To conscience go in quiet mood,
    And find yourself each morn anew;
Feed thou upon the psychic food
    That makes the gods in mortal hue:
This is the way that men are great—
    All those who smile with Nature's laws
So then, why brood and curse your fate?
    Brace up and strike against your flaws!

October 26, 1927

The Little Minds

The little minds that're in the world you know
    Are makers of most troubles that you see;
So small in vision they will ever sow
    Confusion over land and foreign sea:
In politics they reign supreme and great,
    To fool the innocent and rob their rights,
Thus spreading o'er the land vile human hate,
    To end in death and wasteful battle flights.

So selfish are the politicians now
    That neither soul nor body need not hope,
If to their ways and schemes you do not bow
    With cheer, to fall in line with party dope:
These rascals have hand the right of way,
    So gained by fraud and many studied tricks,
And then, to keep the populace at bay,
    They threaten all good men with "legal bricks."

No wonder then the world is gone to hell,
    For good men have no place to move nor sit;
This needs no vision of a William Tell,
    For you can feel or look just straight at it:
A wonderful reform for all must be,
    To save the world for good, and make men right;
There must be liberty for you and me,
    For this, all sober minds should strive and fight.

October 26, 1927

The Bearers

We are the bearers of the world's bright torch
    To light our civilization as we go:
No one should fall or lodge at darkness' porch;
Right well we teach the people all to know:
    There's much for us to do in toil of love,
In helping others as we climb the heights;
    It is for us to reach and lift above
Those who are struggling up through gloomy nights.

Our beaming standard is the Cross of Christ,
    The same that Simon bore, and fainted not;
Up through the age we will this emblem hoist,
    To falter neither a tittle nor a jot:
The cause of men is dear to us alway;
    For right and truth we stand, most firm, as one.
And so we'll battle on from day today,
    In fighting for the noble aims of man.

'Tis true the world is reckless, vile and tough;
    But there is always room for doing good:
There never can of goodness be enough,
    In blessing Nature's wanton brotherhood;
Will you now join the faithful, sturdy band,
    To make a better home for man to live?
Will you now stretch to me the other hand,
    And state—"As freely I receive, I give?"

October 26, 1927

Have Faith in Self

Today I made myself in life anew,
    By going to that royal fount of truth,
And searching for the secret of the few
    Whose goal in life and aim is joy forsooth.
I found at last the friend and counsellor
    That taught me all that I in life should know;
It is the soul, the sovereign chancellor,
    The guide and keeper of the good you sow.

I am advised—"Go ye, have faith in self,
    And seek once more the guide that lives in you"—
Much better than the world of sordid pelf,
    Alas! I found the counsel to be true.
Aha! I know right now that I shall see
    The good in life, and be a better man;
I will by thought and deed pull all to me,
    In saving others, yea, everyone.

Go down and search yourself awhile in part,
    And tell me all of what you see and hear;
Isn't there something pulling at your heart?
    Tell me the truth and have ye then no fear!
There is a voice that speaks to man, within,
    It is the Soul that longs for you to know
There is no need for you to grope in sin,
    For you in truth and light may ever grow.

October 27, 1927

The Last Farewell

Goodbye, my friend, in death we part,
    To meet in realms more glorious:
A void I feel deep in my heart,
    For much there was of love in us:
To see you go is awful pain,
    For thou hast been a world to me;
But we shall meet for good again,
    To see the light that hallows thee.

This death is only transient;
    It leads to brighter and new vales,
So wonderful, munificent,
    As prophets tell in holy tales:
Go thou and wait for me a while,
    And rest at God's fair borderland,
There with the angels you will smile,
    In welcome to the saintly band.

Goodbye, my love, my truest friend;
    All else in life for me to do
Was done ere I in grief attend
    To say the last farewell to you:
The sod has covered you from view,
    But memory dear shall linger still,
And I shall think in heart more true
    Of all your good, and not of ill.

October 27, 1927

Why Disconsolate?

Oh, traveler, disconsolate!
    Thine heart may yet in solace be,
So brood ye not as if from Fate
    Ignoble thou canst not be free.
Let's journey to the heights of love,
    And cast behind the fears of death;
There is no death in life above,
    For man is truly spiritual breath.

You are an entity of Grace
    Divine, yes, partly God in One:
Your image is divine in race,
    Although you may be mortal man.
Go seek the knowledge of the law,
    Go make yourself the lord of earth;
See then the light that Moses saw,
    That gave him vision of this worth!

To be yourself in triumph great,
    You must the world in truth subdue:
Stamp out the evil thought of fate,
    And manly courage then pursue:
The vineyards of the world are yours;
    Go ye and have your rightful share,
For Nature opened all her doors
    To you, in love, beyond compare.

October 29, 1927

Let Us Know

O, thou profound, eternal blue,
    God's mystic arch of heaven-land!
Art thou not veiling spirit hue,
    And hiding the angelic band?
Jehovah! so move this veil,
That we may see the throne of light.
From which St. Gabriel brought the "Hail"
    To Mary, on that Holy night!

We've slumbered much in darkness here,
    And now we seek more light from Thee:
We feel that peace is reigning there—
    Beyond the clouds, o'er land and sea.
The mystery of eternal life
Provokes the soul's sad tedium;
    We faint beneath this mortal strife,
And long to join the angels' hum.

Forgive us, Lord, if we have erred,
    In asking this before our time;
We only sought the light, and aired
    Our souls to tunes of spiritual rhyme;
For death has been a puzzle here;
    Some say we live forever on,
Some say we go from life nowhere;
    To tell us right, Thou art the One!

We wait on Thee, great God above!
    But let the message come today:
We sing Thy praise, and Thee we love,
    As to Thee, Father, do we pray:

Let Michael come in glory great,
    To teach us all that we should do;
And then we'll know our rightful fate,
    In worship to the Son and You.

October 29, 1927

Love's Morning Star

I've waited patiently for you,
    And now you come to make me glad;
I shall be ever good and true,
    And be the dearest, sweetest dad.

You cheer my life with every smile,
    And make me feel much like a bird
That flits and sings just all the while
    Such songs as you have always heard.

You are the beacon light, my dear,
    That guides me on the happy way;
Such love as yours I would not share,
    But treasure in my heart all day.

I dream of you each eve and morn;
    I picture you from distance far,
And everywhere, where love is born,
    You are the brightest morning star.

October 31, 1927

WHITE AND BLACK

The white man held the blacks as slaves,
And bled their souls in living death;
Bishops and priests, and kings themselves,
Preached that the law was right and just;
And so the people worked and died,
And crumbled into material dust.
Good God! The scheme is just the same
Today, between the black and white
Races of men, who gallop after fame.
Can'st Thou not change this bloody thing,
And make white people see the truth
That over blacks must be their king,
Not white, but of their somber hue,
To rule a nation of themselves?

October 31, 1927

THE LOVE AMIE

(Dedicated to Mrs. Amy Jacques Garvey)

I wandered far in life's stern way
To seek the good of everyday;
But fell among the thieves of Thane,
Who tried to rob my honest name.

I found no brotherhood in man;
But here and there a vicious clan;
No truth, no love, no justice find
Their way into these groups unkind.

But you have been a light to me,
A fond and dear, and true Amie;
So what care I for falsest friend,
When on your love I can depend.

To steal one's wealth is always trash,
O'er which some men are ne'er abash;
But then to steal and blot a name,
It takes the courage of a Thane.

But all they do is only nought,
Because the battle has been fought,
And I have won your love, Amie,
The greatest treasure I can see.

October 31, 1927

The Start

Today I start my life for good;
    I am determined now to find
The value of my real manhood;
    And not to travel as if blind.
I am yet young in age and hope;
    I shall so think and do aright,
Things human, and, all in my scope,
    To make of life a shining light.

There shall be no mistake in plan,
    For time does not permit to lose,
And win again, the race of man;
    Hence, now I start, and rightly choose.
I shall not travel wild to find
    That I have fallen almost flat,
Then rise to weep and leave behind
    That I a coward was for that.

So find yourself in early age,
    To know what you shall be in life;
Then go and write on hist'ry's page
    The vict'ries of your daily strife;
For every man is battling you,
    To cross the plain, with haste to win
And hoist the flag in colors blue—
    Then show the world where he has been.

October 31, 1927

Death's Pleasure

Death is no terror, friend!
  It's a sublime sleep
That lulls the weary home
  To rest—not to weep:
It is the solace of God—
  A message for you
From those friends, gone before,
  Those whose love is true.

The dream called death is not
  The pain that you fear;
It's an ecstacy
  Beyond man's compare;
'Tis life's joy—that's called
  The Eternal Fair.

November 10, 1927

Vision of Niagara

I stood at Niagara's Falls today,
    And viewed the wond'rous work of God;
The mighty river flowing by right o'way,
    Yes, dashing o'er the shaking sod.

I looked again at Nature, and I saw
    That God was everywhere in view:
The roaring river was of ancient law,
    Like sun, and moon and stars-not new.

I learnt a valued lesson then and there,
    To see the waters fall below,
For every drop was like a human tear
    Thus shed in earthly passion's flow.

At once I tossed my head above to look,
    To read the story of the sky;
It was so plain—this Nature's open book—
    I could not doubt, there was no Why!
Again I looked with conscience, easy,
At Niagara's angry surge—
A living duplicate of Zambezi,
That beats time's funeral dirge.

And then I knew that all of life is one,
    A march from cradle to the grave:
That every atom is a part of man,
    Who passes—coward and the brave.

November 13, 1927

THE BATTLE HYMN OF AFRICA

Africa's sun is shining above the horizon clear,
The day for us is rising, for black men far and near;
Our God is in the front line, the heav'nly batallion leads,
Onward, make your banners shine, ye men of noble deeds.

There's a flag we love so well—
The red, the black and green,
Greatest emblem tongues can tell,
The brightest ever seen.

When pandemonium breaks, the earth will tremble fast,
Nor oceans, seas nor lakes shall save the first or last;
Our suffering has been long, our cries to God ascending;
We have counted ev'ry wrong which calls for an amending.

So into battle let us go, with the Cross before;
The Angels, great, from high to low, watch forevermore;
We see the enemy scatter, and watch their ranks divide—
With God there is no fetter for whom He doth provide.

All God's children, in trouble, or burdened down with care,
No matter where, how humble, His love is ever there;
So cheerful let our courage be and rally for the King,
The Saviour, Christ, the Lord, is He, whom angels tidings bring.

Ho, Africa, victorious! See, the foe goes down!
The Christ and Simon lead us to wear the triumphant crown;
Jesus remembers dearly the sacrifice with the cross,
So raise those banners gladly—never to suffer loss!

And so the war is ending, the victor's palm is ours,
Crushed 'neath a sorry bending, like dead, fallen flowers
Thus lay the proud men of the day, all lost, forever,
Where the demons never say to God, "We'll deliver."

The Dividing Line

There's a dividing line, call it what you may,
It separates the whites from the blacks each day.
Nature made no passing, shadowy blunder
When by race different people set asunder.
You may try to patch a broken fence between,
But one oneness of aim shall e'er be seen;
For peace and happiness, it is the best,
To group them nationally, one from the rest.

Angels are separated by groups and files,
Not because of superiority in lives,
But to maintain heavenly rule and order,
As desired by the Great, Holy Father.
So in this physical, material life
We are thus separated to prevent strife;
Not because we are better than the other,
But for the sake of others not to bother.

Everyone should obey this grand human rule,
And not others to reduce to our footstool.
Justice should be for everyone we meet,
As with charity and fellowship we greet.
This would make a better and happier world
With the banner of peace and love unfurled.
No fair mortal man can think this unkind
If he appreciates the bond of mankind.

HAIL! UNITED STATES OF AFRICA!

Hail! United States of Africa-free!
Hail! Motherland most bright, divinely fair!
State in perfect sisterhood united,
Born of truth; mighty thou shalt ever be.

Hail! Sweet land of our father's noble kin!
Let joy within thy bounds be ever known;
Friend of the wandering poor, and helpless, thou,
Light to all, such as freedom's reigns within.

From Liberia's peaceful western coast
To the foaming Cape at the southern end,
There's but one law and sentiment sublime,
One flag, and its emblem of which we boast.

The Nigerias are all united now,
Sierra Leone and the Gold Coast, too.
Gambia, Senegal, not divided,
But in one union happily bow.

The treason of the centuries is dead,
All alien whites are forever gone;
The glad home of Sheba is once more free,
As o'er the world the black man raised his head.

Bechuanaland, a State with Kenya,
Members of the Federal Union grand,
Send their greetings to sister Zanzibar,
And so does laughing Tanganyika.

Over in Grand Mother Mozambique,
The pretty Union Flag floats in the air,
She is sister to good Somaliland,
Smiling with the children of Dahomey.

Three lusty cheers for old Basutoland,
Timbuctoo, Tunis and Algeria,
Uganda, Kamerun, all together
Are in the Union with Nyasaland.

We waited long for fiery Morocco,
Now with Guinea and Togo she has come,
All free and equal in the sisterhood,
Like Swazi, Zululand and the Congo.

There is no state left out of the Union—
The East, West, North, South, including Central,
Are in the nation, strong forever,
Over blacks in glorious dominion.

Hail! United States of Africa-free!
Country of the brave black man's liberty;
State of greater nationhood thou hast won,
A new life for the race is just begun.

Africa for the Africans

Say! Africa for the Africans,
Like America for the Americans:
This the rallying cry for a nation,
Be it in peace or revolution.

Blacks are men, no longer cringing fools;
They demand a place, not like weak tools;
But among the world of nations great
They demand a free self-governing state.

Hurrah! Hurrah! Great Africa wakes;
She is calling her sons, and none forsakes,
But to colors of the nation runs,
Even though assailed by enemy guns.

Cry it loud, and shout it long, hurrah!
Time has changed, so hail! New Africa!
We are now awakened, rights to see;
We shall fight for dearest liberty.

Mighty kingdoms have been truly reared
On the bones of black men, facts declared;
History tells this awful, pungent truth,
Africa awakes to her rights forsooth.

Europe cries to Europeans, ho!
Asiatics claim Asia, so
Australia for Australians,
And Africa for the Africans.

Black men's hands have joined now together,
They will fight and brave all death's weather,
Motherland to save, and make her free,
Spreading joy for all to live and see.

None shall turn us back, in freedom's name,
We go marching like to men of fame
Who have given laws and codes to kings,
Sending evil flying on crippled wings.

Black men shall in groups reassemble,
Rich and poor and the great and humble:
Justice shall be their rallying cry,
When millions of soldiers pass us by.

Look for that day, coming, surely soon,
When the sons of Ham will show no coon
Could the mighty deeds of valor do
Which shall bring giants for peace to sue.

Hurrah! Hurrah! Better times are near;
Let us front the conflict and prepare;
Greet the world as soldiers, bravely true:
"Sunder not," Africa shouts to you.

A Note About the Author

Marcus Garvey (1887–1940) was a controversial yet influential political activist, entrepreneur and journalist. Born in Saint Ann's Bay, Jamaica, Garvey experienced first hand the ills of colonialism, colorism and racism during his upbringing, ultimately shaping his view of the world. His early adult years were spent learning trades and involving himself in political organizations such as The National Club and going onto create the United Negro Improvement Association and the African Communities League in 1914. Three years after this, he would go onto the United States, with the hopes of further expanding the U.N.I.A and spreading his message of Black brotherhood in an "Africa for Africans," spilling into the creation of a weekly newspaper, The Negro World in 1918. As Garveyism began to take hold in Black communities in the United States and abroad, Garvey faced increased government surveillance and strife as he attempted to branch out into other ventures like *The Black Star Line*. Between 1922–1925, Garvey was arrested and tried on accusations of mail fraud before his eventual deportation from the United States in 1927. Never one to become settled, Garvey lived out the rest of his life attempting to travel the world and continue to spread his ideology; while often clashing with other Black leaders and organizations of the time. A very complicated and complex figure, Garvey was nevertheless an important piece to the foundation of Black nationalism as it is known today.

A Note from the Publisher

Spanning many genres, from non-fiction essays to literature classics to children's books and lyric poetry, Mint Edition books showcase the master works of our time in a modern new package. The text is freshly typeset, is clean and easy to read, and features a new note about the author in each volume. Many books also include exclusive new introductory material. Every book boasts a striking new cover, which makes it as appropriate for collecting as it is for gift giving. Mint Edition books are only printed when a reader orders them, so natural resources are not wasted. We're proud that our books are never manufactured in excess and exist only in the exact quantity they need to be read and enjoyed. To learn more and view our library, go to minteditionbooks.com

bookfinity & MINT EDITIONS

Enjoy more of your favorite classics with Bookfinity,
a new search and discovery experience for readers.
With Bookfinity, you can discover more vintage
literature for your collection, find your Reader Type,
track books you've read or want to read,
and add reviews to your favorite books.
Visit www.bookfinity.com, and click on
Take the Quiz to get started.

Don't forget to follow us
@bookfinityofficial and @mint_editions